ISBN: 978129034959


Published by:
HardPress Publishing
8345 NW 66TH ST #2561
MIAMI FL 33166-2626

Email: info@hardpress.net
Web: http://www.hardpress.net

*BY THE SAME AUTHOR.*

# THE BOOK OF ISAIAH.

*In Two Volumes.*

Vol. I. Chaps. 1 to 39.      Vol. II. Chaps. 40 to 66.

Crown 8vo, cloth, price 7s. 6d. each.

LONDON : HODDER AND STOUGHTON.

# THE PREACHING

## OF THE

# OLD TESTAMENT TO THE AGE

BY

## GEORGE ADAM SMITH, M.A.

*Professor of Hebrew in the Free Church College, Glasgow*

London

## HODDER AND STOUGHTON

27, PATERNOSTER ROW

MDCCCXCIII

ANUEL

JR

8267

THIS Lecture was delivered as an Inaugural Address on the author's induction to the Chair of Hebrew and Old Testament Exegesis in the Free Church College, Glasgow. Some personal allusions have been omitted, some paragraphs which were omitted in delivery have been retained, and some notes have been added.

FATHERS AND BRETHREN, FELLOW STUDENTS,—The present condition of Old Testament science offers many opportunities for such a general review as forms the usual subject of an inaugural address. For a long time past, every relevant science, every possible school of belief, have shot across the Old Testament their opposing lights, under which there has been the most extraordinary exercise of individual labour and ingenuity. It is commonplace to say that no other literature of equal size has been so fully explored and debated. And the result is that to-day there may be reached, almost everywhere upon it, points of view from which we can survey what is already settled, and prospect the inevitable directions of our advance across what is not.

I feel, however, that to a beginner like myself these points of view form temptations rather than opportunities, and that to-day it would be better if I gave you something within my own experience—the rather that this coincides with what is, after all, the main purpose of the Old Testament through us who are its students.

It has been the custom of the Church of Scotland to call to the chairs of her colleges, those who have already been practical preachers of God's Word. In this way, of course, the interests of scholarship have been set at some disadvantage —

seldom discounted even by the numerous opportunities of science which the Church offers to her students before their entrance upon the ministry. But, on the other hand, as we all recognise with gratitude, the system effectually prevents both professors and students from forgetting that the final end of our colleges is the equipment of preachers of God's Word and pastors of His people—that in them the . most perfect scholarship of which we are capable is indeed to be coveted earnestly, along with all other best gifts, but only for the sake of the practical ministry of the Church both at home and abroad. And for myself, I should like to say that if my call to this chair were a call away from practical work, I would not be here. I have not left a pulpit, which I loved and found freedom in, for any other ultimate purpose than the one for which the Church sent me to it, or with any other confidence than that the free and full study of the Old Testament by teachers and scholars together, has for its inevitable result the preaching of God's simple Word to the people.

In harmony with these considerations, I propose to take as the subject of this address—

## THE PREACHING OF THE OLD TESTAMENT TO THE AGE.

### I.

But, *first*, let us look back upon the place which the Old Testament has taken in Christian preaching down to the present day.

1. For us preachers of Christ, the supreme
sanction of the Old Testament is that
which it received from Himself. The Old
Testament was the Bible of Jesus Christ—
the Bible of His education and the Bible
of His ministry. He grew out of the
Old Testament, and He taught His
disciples to recognise Him in it. He in-
terpreted it by His word, and justified
its hopes and claims by His work ; but
conversely He used it to justify His own
mission, and to light up the mystery of
His cross. He repealed, indeed, some of its
strongest tempers and institutions ; He
added to it beyond all its own dreams.
But on the other side, how much in it
He took for granted ; how much He
enforced ; how much He came expressly
to fulfil ! He took for granted all its
fundamental doctrines about man, about

creation, about righteousness ; about God's providence of the world, and about His method of grace through Israel. He accepted its history as a preparation for Himself. He drew from it most of the categories of His gospel. He enforced its righteousness and vindicated its spirituality, especially by using it as an argument for the ´ spiritual character of His own mission. But above all, He fed His own soul upon it, and expressly set Himself to the fulfilment of its calls and its ideals. These are the highest external proofs— if we can call them external—for the abiding validity of the Old Testament in the life and work of Christ's Church.

2. We next find the Old Testament employed in all departments of their preaching, apologetic and ethical, by the Apostles. Even those of the Apostles, who

most emphasise the expiry of the Old Dispensation, are ready to draw from its Scriptures proofs of the Divine mission of Christ, truths about Creation and Providence, examples of character, aids to worship.

And all this was not only for the Jew : a little reflection will show us that in practical religion the Old Testament was equally indispensable to the Gentile. He also needed a cosmogony, and a history of God's dealings with the race from the beginning, in harmony with his new faith. He also needed proof for the argument that Jesus was the Christ. Indeed the question, why the Son of Man was born a Jew, pressed upon the Gentile with a force unfelt by Jews themselves ; and the answer to that question was to be found only in the Old Testament. Moreover, the Gentile,

a judge impartial and uncommitted, dis-
cerned the spirituality of the Old Testament.   He found that the Law quickened
also his conscience, and that the Psalter
uttered also his experience.   Thus, inde-
pendently of Jewish dogma or canon of
Scripture, the Gentile Church adopted the
Old Testament altogether for the sake of
her Lord and for the sake of herself.   In
her argument she learned, that whosoever
will reckon with Jesus Christ must reckon
with the Old Testament ; for her own life
she proved the virtue of those sources from
which her Lord had nourished His.   In
Christian philosophy and Christian worship
the place of the Old Testament was thus
secure from the beginning, for reasons both
logical and practical.

3. Among other proofs of how widely such
motives extended the acceptance of the Old

Testament across early Christendom, we may mention four. *First*, the same anxiety was evinced by the Church to determine the limits of the Old Testament canon as to determine those of the New.[1] *Second*, there was the remarkable rejection of the Old Testament by so many of the heresies—a consequence of the narrow vision and impatient intellect which counted its difficulties irreconcilable with each other or with the Gospel.[2] *Thirdly*, there was the frequent use of Old Testament character and narrative in popular preaching all over the Church ; from which we may infer, either as cause or result, a familiarity with the Old Testament on the part of the common people. And, *fourthly*, there was the influence of the Mosaic Law upon legislation and public morals, which

[1] Buhl on the Canon of the O. T., Eng. trans., p. 50.
[2] Marcion, many of the Gnostics, the Cainites, &c.

began with Constantine, and from his time
to Justinian's purged social life and modified
the law of Rome.[1]   To these proofs of the
spread of the Old Testament we may, perhaps, add a fifth—the readiness with which,
later on, the young Christian nations of
Europe found in the history of the Jewish
people parallels for their own struggles to
freedom.

4. Along all the lines I have indicated,
the preaching of the Old Testament has
been sustained through the centuries to the
present day.   Of course it has suffered alike
from the temporary fashions of exegesis
and the abiding sins of the preacher.   The
spoiled children of the pulpit were let
loose on the Old Testament as they were
upon the New, and in its wider range and

[1] Gibbon's chapter on Roman Jurisprudence, vol.
v. of Smith's edition, p. 197, &c.

more obscure circumstance took a proportionally larger license :—the allegorist, who could spin his eighty sermons out of the first chapter of the Song of Solomon ; 'the mere flatterer of Jesus Christ, as we may well call him, who without moral insight or real devotion, heaped upon our Lord indiscriminately all the titles of the Old Testament and symbolised every detail of Jewish life and fashion, as if it were the ingenuity of his efforts and the quantity of his results that were well-pleasing to God ; the bigot who claimed the relentlessness of the old law as sanction for his own cruelties to Christ's little flock ; and the dry official, with his fixed hours to fill, to whom the Old Testament was chiefly welcome for its quantity, and who week by week cut from it his tedious lengths before unmoved congregations.

2

But, on the other hand, down all these ages true inspiration has been drawn from the Old Testament by reasonable defenders of Christ against both Jew and infidel ; by real prophets, who knew the spirituality and holy passion of the great examples of their order ; by mystics, to whose pure hearts the ancient pages glowed with a vision of God, denied to mere ingenuity and official zeal; by experimental preachers, who, moving through that rich old world of character, won insight and force and freedom, unattainable elsewhere ; and by social reformers, to whose noble line Europe owes an almost ceaseless application of the principles of Hebrew prophecy to the generations of her public life.

5. It is this last use of the Old Testament which, next to preaching Christ Himself, has predominated in Western Christendom.[1]

[1] This is almost as true of Eastern Christendom from the fourth to the sixth centuries. The greatest

From the time that the example of the Pentateuch affected Roman law,[1] and braced the rulers of the empire to grapple with at least the bestial sins, the Old Testament has done its Divine share in inspiring both the reformers of public morals and the defenders of the rights of the people. We forget, for instance, that Savonarola, besides reviving a pure Gospel, was a great preacher of civic righteousness : he became so by his lectures upon Amos and other prophetical books. From his day to our own there never was a European city or nation moved to higher ideals of justice and charity, without the reawakening of those ancient voices which declared to Jacob his sin

preacher of the East, Chrysostom, by expositions and homilies applied the O. T. to the life of his day in the most practical spirit.

[1] Gibbon, ibid.

and to Israel his transgression. It is enough for us to remember, in our own country, the earlier Puritans, like Henry Smith with his "Scripture for Magistrates" and his "Memento for Magistrates;" the later Puritans like Goodwin, whose sermons to the House of Commons and on public occasions were nearly always upon Old Testament texts ;[1] and the revival of this kind of preaching, adapted to modern life, by Kingsley and Maurice — Maurice, who (in his own words) counted "paramount the duty of vindicating the Old Testament as the great witness for liberty ; . . . the witness of the sacredness of this earth."[2]

But outside sermons, take the great suc-

[1] Carlyle's *Cromwell's Letters and Speeches*, iv., cf. pp. 19 and 21. Cromwell himself was fond of preaching from the O. T., and (to use his own phrase) its "recapitulation of Providence."

[2] Life, ii., p. 490 ; cf. 452, 454, &c.

cession of treatises, which form an almost complete history of the political ideal in Europe from Constantine to the period immediately before the French Revolution. Augustine's *De Civitate Dei;* Dante's *De Monarchia;* the political tracts of the German reformers ; Milton's *Defence of the People of England ;* our own Buchanan's *De Jure Regni apud Scotos ;* Rutherford's *Lex Rex.* By all of these the Old Testament is used ; and by some used lavishly. It is a fact of great interest, that in the prodigious controversy between the Divine Right of Kings and the Liberty of the People, the advocates of the former chiefly chose texts from the New Testament ; while the champions of the people relied on the Old. Our own royalist divines used as their proof-texts for the sacredness of the Stuart House Pilate's words to Christ, *I have power to crucify or release thee ;* Paul's, *the powers that be are ordained of God;* Peter's, *the King as supreme.* Whereas the Scriptures, which, after the fashion of the times, popular champions like Milton and Rutherford preferred against them, are all drawn from the Old Testament—from the narratives of the election of Saul and David, from the part played by the people in the coronation of the later kings, from the subjection of the kings to the covenant, as well as from many passages of the prophets. When we read chapter on chapter of such arguments, and remember that the Book from which they were drawn was already in the hands and hearts of the common people, we appreciate how much of the liberty, which these wonderful centuries secured to us, is due to the Old Testament.

It is obvious that the distinction between the Old and New Testament, which this controversy emphasised, is no artificial one. The political circumstances of the two dispensations were entirely different. Through Old Testament history we follow the growth, the opportunities, the judgment of a nation. The purpose of God is a people ; religious discipline and experience, religious duty and hope, are almost entirely identified with national rights and responsibilities, the struggle for national liberty and national righteousness. But in the New Testament we do not deal with a nation at all. It is an entirely exceptional state of affairs; in which religion neither is associated with popular struggles, nor assumes the responsibilities of government, but the sole political duty of the believer is reverence to the powers that be—the guardians of the Providential Peace in which the Church of Christ was to spread across the world. This is a state of affairs not so like modern history as the other was ; and therefore it is, that in this one province of religion the Hebrew prophets have been felt by the moderns to stand nearer to them than the apostles do. The apostles were sojourners and pilgrims ; the prophets were citizens and patriots. And I may add, therefore it is that the Old Testament, though of course upon a plane of public life different from that on which our forefathers applied it, must always have a function to discharge supplementary to the more glorious function of the New Testament. To this I shall presently recur.

6. This main use of the Old Testament sustained through so many centuries, carries us down to modern preaching. Here let us take a wider survey. Upon this latest stretch of history, over these crowded areas of Western life, do the voices ring less clear from that ancient, Eastern coast? On the contrary,

there has been no time in which the Old Testament has been more studied, no life to the problems of which its principles have been applied with more confidence.

The great preachers of the last century and a half have, with one exception, derived much of the force and charm of their preaching from the Old Testament. That exception is Schleiermacher, who as a preacher would have nothing to do with the Old Testament, judging it to stand to Christianity in the same relation as Paganism. "For our ethics," he said, "the Old Testament is entirely superfluous." Rothe has exposed the historical injustice of these views; and they have met with their penalty. As Dr. John Ker says: "One cannot but see that Schleiermacher's style has suffered from his neglect of the Old Testament." With this single exception the great preachers of recent times have largely drawn from the Old Testament, and no preaching has been received with more delight by the common people. Much of the attraction is due, of course, to the variety and picturesqueness of the Old Testament, to its lyric elements, to the gallant and heroic in it, and to the warm patriotism in which its religion is so often incarnate. But apart from these, the modern mind is especially drawn to the Old Testament, by its portraiture of character, its ideals of social righteousness, its vision of history as the tribunal of God, its treatment of speculative questions, and its treatment of the prudential aspects of life—neither of which last two is treated by the New Testament in detail. Above all, it is the Old Testament's inimitable portraiture of character upon which our great preachers have combined. Men of such different schools as

Sterne—for the author of *Tristram Shandy* was also among the prophets—Butler, Foster, Newman, Spurgeon, Robertson of Brighton, Maurice, our own Candlish and Arnot—have all been brilliant and effective upon the heroes and villains of Hebrew story. Who does not remember how searching Butler is on Balaam, how impressive Newman is upon Saul ? Sterne's sermons, which he characteristically offers to his fashionable subscribers as ' a few reflections on the present state of society'— and, by the way, though very discursive, Sterne's sermons repay reading for their unconventional style and frequent fitness of phrase—are inimitable exposures of the weakness of that nature, which patriarchs, prophets, and kings shared with ourselves. Robertson's strong moral sense and power of analysis found full scope in the Old Testament—busy especially to trace the endlessness of sin, and to illustrate that the Divine forgiveness does not necessarily remove the earthly consequences of our faults. But he is always finest on the difference that Christ has made—the difference in ideals of duty, in hope, in the meaning and efficacy of the basal institutions of human life—marriage, the family, and the state. Maurice, on the other hand, is the obverse of Robertson, emphasising Christ as already present in the Old Testament—the Word which was from the beginning, the Spirit both of the Law and the Prophets. I have already recorded how Maurice and Kingsley revived the social application of the Old Testament. This was for England. For Scotland their example was not required. For more than two centuries the liberties, the patriotism, the proudest memories of the Scottish people had been associated with the institutions and

the heroisms of Old Testament history. It
was not only that the prevailing theology in
Scotland conceived of God's relation to man
under the form of a covenant; but, as in
Israel's case, the covenant was a national one,
and comprised every public interest. The
Scottish preachers, who in times of persecu-
tion taught their suffering nation to see herself in the Trampled Vine, the Desolate City,
and the Remnant of God's pity and promise;
in times of peace and construction enforced
upon every department of her life the whole
righteousness of ancient Israel. Nor was it
that legalism they preached, which, being
falsely imputed to Scotland, has moved
some to call her in scorn 'the Judæa of the
West.' The preachers of the Covenant have
ever kept before the people far more the
Person of their King than the letter of His
Law; it was not legal obedience they de-

manded, but those chivalrous affections which are as the fire to cleanse national life and to kindle a people to sacrifice and service—zeal for the honour of God, loyalty to Christ the King, and the conviction that He is so identified with the poor and oppressed of the people, that no efforts can be too costly for their sakes. And even when Scottish preaching has turned more specially to ethics, it has not been the Law which it has used, so much as the more widely applicable morality of the Books of Wisdom. Indeed, we cannot overestimate the effect, which, at least till a recent date, the regular exposition of the Book of Proverbs, in church and school and home, has exercised upon the Scottish character.

Students—such is your field, and such are your examples!

## II.

" But we," it will be said, " have fallen upon harder times. The rich, confident preaching you have described was all achieved before the influence of modern criticism had reached the pulpit. With perhaps the very slight exception of Maurice,[1] none of the great preachers you have named can be examples to us in the strangely new conditions of Old Testament study. Never before has there been such a crisis in the history of the preaching of the Old Testament ; it is essential for us to know what difference the modern criticism has made, or is likely to make, in the material, the methods, the inspiration for which the Christian pulpit has hitherto looked to the Hebrew Scriptures."

[1] Maurice felt the influence of the great debate raised by Colenso, but was not greatly affected.

It is a fair challenge ; and I will meet it as fully as the limits of this lecture permit. Remember, I am not now giving an opinion, how far the results of modern criticism have been established. I am only dealing with the question, whether there is anything either in these results or in the methods which have produced them, to endanger the practical usefulness of the Old Testament,—to weaken our power of preaching it to the people as the Word of God. This is a practical question, and I trust that the consideration of a few plain facts, about which there can be no controversy, may serve to allay the uneasiness and alarm that have arisen in some quarters.

1. First, the new criticism is not necessarily connected with the rationalism which cuts the sinews of a preacher—the rationalism which before now has emptied the Christian

pulpit of faith and of fire. In this country at the present day nearly every leader in Old Testament criticism—and remember some are as advanced as any on the Continent—is a believer in evangelical Christianity. That being so, it is only fair to ascribe the rationalism of *some* continental critics of the Old Testament to other causes than their conclusions on Hebrew history and the authorship of the Hebrew Scriptures. Ours still affirm the truths which must be the strength of all Christian preaching. The sovereign grace of God to sinful men, the Divinity of our Lord, His atoning death and resurrection, the descent of the Holy Spirit upon the Church—these are held and held heartily by critics among us, the most learned, the most sane, the most free, the most advanced. Or, to speak of truths within the special province of the Old Testament

3

preacher—take the uniqueness of the Old
Testament in the education of the race ; take
the inexplicableness of prophecy by natural
causes ; take the testimony which prophecy
gives of itself as a positive revelation of God
—they have been affirmed and lately re-
affirmed in our midst by the scholar,
whose researches into Semitic religion as
a whole enable him to speak with greatest
authority on the subject.[1]   Take the Old
Testament as a prophecy of Christ : one of
the most scientific studies of Messianic
prophecy in our own or any language affirms
that there is proof of its " true connection
with the Gospel dispensation as part of one
grand scheme in the counsels of Providence."[2]
Take the wider apologetic bearing of the

[1] Professor Robertson Smith in the new edition of
*The Old Testament in the Jewish Church.*

[2] Stanton, *The Jewish Messiah.*

history of Israel as a whole : more than
one critic has offered in corroboration of the
truth of the new theories, the conviction that
they are of greater apologetic value than
were the traditional.[1]    Take Paul's argument
about the relations of law and gospel ; take
our Lord's explanation of the relations between the old law and His own : neither of
these is at all affected by even the ex-
treme conclusions of the school of Graf—
unless, indeed, it be that the latter lends
them new light and force.[2]

2. The second fact which it is well to keep
in mind, is the comparatively small portion
of the preacher's field in the Old Testament
which the newer criticism has disturbed.
Much of the historical narrative, it is true, is
questioned in our day to an extent which

[1] *Old Testament in the Jewish Church, passim.*
[2] Ibid., Lecture xi., especially p. 315 f.

must make the preacher, who reads current
criticism, timid about treating certain characters and events, from which in time
past Christian preaching has drawn much
interest and much spiritual power, both for
young and old.   But the amount of the
history assailed is far less than is ordinarily
supposed.   Many of the passages on which
doubt is thrown are those duplicate narratives, which have always been an em-
barrassment to conscientious preachers : and
elsewhere, the preachers who, reading the
latest criticism, are troubled by the difficulties about the historical character of the
story, will find the ethical resources are as
great, sometimes greater than ever.[1]

Even though such figures as Abraham,
Esau, Jacob, Joseph, Gideon, be presented to

[1] Cheyne, *Aids to the Devout Study of Criticism,*
Part i.

us in narratives, of which it is simply im-
possible for us, at this time of day, to esta-
blish the accuracy, is that to render their
characters and influences of less use to the
preacher? Is that to make it less possible
to employ them, as they are employed in the
Epistle to the Hebrews? I cannot at all see
that it must be so. But the region over
which this doubt is possible is, as I say,
much less than many suppose.

Outside this, consider what great parts
of the Old Testament field of the preacher
remain unquestioned by criticism. Unquestioned? I should rather say, fortified,
explored, made habitable by modern men.
There are the prophets, the books of specu-
lation, the books which apply the fear of
God and the wisdom springing from it to the
everyday life of man. No historical criticism
can affect these fields; across them the

preacher of to-day. may move with all the confidence and undistracted boldness of his fathers—nay, with more freshness, more insight, more agility, for the text is clearer, the allusions better understood, and all the old life re-quickened out of which these books originally sprang.     There remain the Psalms. Even though the proof be made out, that the psalms are not by the individuals, whom Christian preaching has hitherto had in view when using them, how can that diminish their value to the preacher ?     It cannot detract from their character as expressions of the authentic experience of the Church under every possible condition of life and of death ; it cannot impair their exhaustless inspiration both of prayer and of prophecy. If it robs them of some of the picturesque circumstance often so useful to the preacher, we must remember that it also relieves him

from those conjectures and imaginations—
that mere confectionery of the pulpit—which
too often have spoiled alike his art and the
appetite of his people for the pure milk of
the word.

### III.

And now let us look at our material itself,
and ask what are the chief contributions
which the Old Testament makes to Christian
preaching.

1. Students,—In returning to the divinity
hall after a ministry of ten years, perhaps
the thing that I have most on my heart to
tell you about the life to which you look
forward—for it is the thing about which, at
your stage, I knew least, and for which I
was least prepared—is the great intellectual

strain of it.   Part of your ministry is the preparation of at least two addresses or sermons a week, year in and year out.   Yours is a duty to a congregation possibly of all kinds of sympathy, of all stages of culture ; it is a routine which, however spiritual is the temper with which you pursue it, can be preserved from weariness and inanity only by constantly furnishing it with fresh subjects of thought, fresh experiences, fresh styles of enforcing the truth.   What resources, what device and change of subjects, does the regular preaching of the Word require !   It is because of this, when I look back to-day upon ten years of preaching, that the first feeling in my heart is one of gratitude to God for the variety of this Book ; this Book, which is not a book, but a literature ; this literature, which is not literature, but life,—full, real, unflattered life upon every level where it has been given to men to suffer, to love, to doubt, to aspire. Gentlemen, you cannot know now ; but some day, when the first weariness comes down upon you, the first subtle fears that you have exhausted, not your gospel, but your ability to preach the gospel—you will then know what it is to have at your command all that rich land where the points of view of the kingdom of God are so numerous and so fresh. What ministry can be monotonous, which not only has this long history, this rich world of characters, these aspects of nature and of the human heart at its disposal, but is spent also in the infection of so many different styles of thought, so many different kinds of temperament !

2. This leads me to consider the living aids which the Old Testament contributes to the preacher's style. I think we all feel the

truth in Dr. Ker's judgment of Schleiermacher's style—"that it suffered from his
neglect of the Old Testament." An old
German writer has said that " Holy Scripture
should be our grammar and our dictionary,
out of which all the modes of Christian
speech should grow." This is true advice,
provided we fulfil it, not in the letter, but in
the spirit : not in the servile and barren
repetition of Bible texts, whether in preaching
or praying ; but in the imitation of those
tempers and affections, which mould the
style of the sacred writers, and of that labour
which they put forth upon their art. What
may we not learn from prophet, psalmist,
and, historian—as to conciseness ; as to the
worth of phrase ; as to concreteness in our
teaching ; as to the inspiration of the events
and circumstances of our ordinary life ; as to
the duty of calling things by their right

names ; as to the effort to bring grace and music into what we say ; as to the urgency which is upon all living truth, and the passion to win men which is the spring of all preaching. What preacher, who is a student of the Old Testament, can fail to be infected by the courage of the prophets, and by their downright realism—a courage and a realism which, I may say in passing, are frequently disguised in our English version ; but the careful student of the original discovers them, and they thrill him to the heart. Gentlemen, do not believe that the end of an accurate study of the Hebrew language is simply familiarity with a number of grammatical forms, more or less obscure. Painstaking students are otherwise rewarded. It is they who lay their hands on the prophet's heart and feel it beat ; it is they who, across the ages, see the very features of his face as he calls ; it is they into whom his style and his music pass.

But the fountain of Old Testament preaching is the passion to win men. This is the secret both of the pathos and the splendours of its style. We know, how to the prophets preaching was no mere display, but a sore battle with the hard hearts of men, in which the preacher worked with the pity of his weakness upon him, at a supreme cost to himself, and ever conscious that he must summon to his desperate task every resource of feeling and of art. Remember Wisdom as she is pictured to us in the Book of Proverbs—not abstract and impersonal, yielding neither help nor sympathy to the few with strength to pursue her, but personal, incarnate, and very fair ; seeking before she is sought ; more urgent and beautiful than our sin, more frequent and obvious than our temptations ; stretching out her hands to men ; crying aloud in the street, uttering her voice in the broad places ; winsome, affectionate, pleading ; passing through the midst of man's common life with the common people's language on her lips. She, the partner of God, the inspiration of the universe, rejoices in the habitable part of the earth, and breaks with joy and gladness upon the sons of men —in all the beauty of art and yet in all the homeliness of their own common tongue, till men say unto her, " Thou art my sister, and unto understanding thou art my kinswoman." This is the Wisdom Who breathes through the whole Old Testament. Her joy you see in its art and eloquence, but the passion of Her heart you find in its yearning to win men for God and for righteousness.

Oh, students ! how can the men be dull and listless, how can they be lax and slovenly, whose professional studies are these, and these their daily companions !

3. I pass now from the question of style to that of subjects. Our rapid historical sketch has already indicated to us the various aspects of religion which form the special province of the Old Testament in Christian preaching. They are first those truths which the New Testament takes for granted, such as the origin of the world and of man ; certain aspects of the Divine character and providence, which require the great ·length and continuity of Old Testament history for their display ; the preparation for Christ, which is also an argument for His· Divinity ; the unfulfilled prophecies of the kingdom of God, of which I have said in another place that the unfulfilled

prophecies of the Old Testament remain the conscience of Christianity ; the religious use of nature, which, though enforced in the New Testament, is illustrated chiefly in psalm and prophecy ; the speculative side of faith, as we have it in Job and Ecclesiastes ; the argument as to suffering ; the treatment of the prudential aspects of human life ; the social and political work of the Holy Spirit ; and finally, all that array of inimitable characters in the drama of Israel's history. The mere list of these is enough to prove the abiding validity and indispensableness of the Old Testament for Christian preaching. I do not venture to examine them all in detail, but will conclude with exemplifying two or three.

4. As to the individual characters, there is no part of the Old Testament which has been more helpful to Christian preaching ;

there is none which has been more abused. It has been abused by employing - those characters in illustration of some utterly irrelevant doctrine or office of the Christian Church. They can be so employed only after you have killed the real life out of them. How often has one seen an Old Testament character, whom one once knew alive, bound to the chariot wheels of some violent dogmatist and dragged round the whole citadel of Christian theology, till there was as much life left in the battered corpse as in Hector's own ! So I have seen Abner and Joab, for the time styled respectively agnostic and atheist, dumped up and down over the beaten course of a hard creed by a vigorous but un- feeling preacher ; and the tedium of · the process was only relieved by imagining the living Abner, the living Joab, looking on at the performance. On the other hand, if we will go to the characters of the Old Testament as they are, and treat them, not as our dead prey, but as our masters and brothers, whom it is our duty to study with patience and meekness, there is almost no end to the real benefit they shall do us. The careful study of the original narrative, the study of the history of the times, the study of the contemporary monuments, which of late are being discovered in such large numbers, reveal to us that these characters are neither the lay figures nor the mere symbols of doctrine which they are often represented to be by a certain kind of preaching, nor, on the other hand, can they be only mythical heroes— incarnations of a tribe or reflections of natural phenomena—to which some mistaken schools of criticism think to reduce them.

4

There is a vividness, a moral reality, about nearly all of them ; and although they rise amid circumstances that we cannot always explain, and are sometimes surrounded by miracles to which our conscience does not always respond—through all this they stalk unhindered, real characters with life and way upon them, and our hearts leap up to pray and to dare to be able to keep step with them.

5. We have seen that the Old Testament has been the great text for Christian preaching upon public life, and we have found the explanation of this in the fact that for much of the Old Testament the religious unit is the community. It is the nation as a whole with whom God deals—whom He chooses, redeems, judges, and uses for service in the world. Now, great as the part has been which in this

direction the Old Testament has played in Christian preaching in the past, I believe that just here the illustrations of the solidarity of a people, the old enforcement of civic righteousness, of the power of the Holy Ghost in the conduct of public life, of the sacredness of history as a constant judgment by God — that all these will still work through the Christian pulpit with effectiveness on our age. That great inspiration in which our forefathers fought for and won the political and religious liberty of this land, it will still be ours in using our liberty for the building of the City of God among us. But I see also other lines of prophecy as yet scarcely touched, along which Christian preaching may find doctrine and example, to appeal even more practically to the conscience of this generation. The Christian pulpit has scarcely touched the rich materials of that remarkable period of Jewish history, in which the consciousness of the individual becomes more articulate than it has formerly been ; and when he has grown aware of his spiritual independence, God teaches him his relation and his duty to the community. In Israel, the emancipation of the individual took a very different course from that which it held in other nations. In other nations its course was that of a revolt, a revolt against authority, and it is represented by the great historical watchwords of free thought, rights of man, individualism, *laissez faire*. In Israel there was the temptation to this, and there was the overcoming of the temptation in favour of a more glorious issue. We see the evolution, so dramatic, so full of meaning for ourselves, in the life of Jeremiah. By Jeremiah's time the community—which

Isaiah had prophesied should last for ever on
its historical site of Zion, and in its political
form as the kingdom of the house of David,
— was about to be broken up. The individual was left to his own resources ;. it
was a call for each one to save himself.
And to a man like Jeremiah, this leading
of Providence came enforced by a number
of religious considerations. As almost none
before him had known, Jeremiah knew how
God can single out the individual, and in
the secret of his own heart deal with him
intimately, apart from his citizenship or his
priesthood. By temper Jeremiah was intro-
spective, solitary, greatly concerned about
himself. And then the community had de-
served nothing of Jeremiah ; they had re-
fused to listen to him, they had cast him off.
What a conspiracy of temptation was here to
break away from the community, to assert

the duty of a purely selfish religion, to save
one's own soul out of so manifestly doomed
a dispensation ! Jeremiah tells us how he felt
it all ; how at one time he longed to flee to
some lonely lodge in the wilderness, like the
Christian monks of later days; how at another
the Chaldæans gave him the opportunity of
deserting to them. But God showed him
a more excellent way ; and Jeremiah had
scarcely found his rights as an individual,
and his value to God as an individual, before
through heart and conscience he felt his
oneness with the people—a sympathy with
their sufferings, a conscience of their sins,
of which, though it perplexed him, he
could not get rid, and which he gradually
articulated by word and deed into the
chief gospel of his book—*He that loseth
his life shall save it.* Not by breaking from
the community was the individual to realise

himself, but by taking it to his heart, by feeling its sorrows and its sins as if they were his own, and by sharing its misery and even its punishment from God ; in short, by making the community his other self. And this, I take it, is the explanation of the curious individualism of the Psalter, which has lately caused much controversy among us. That entanglement of experience which so puzzles us in most of the Psalms; those cries in which we hear now the conscience of the individual, now the conscience of the community—are due to the feeling that Christ has taught is the deepest and truest of all religion, the feeling of solidarity and sympathy—the vicarious conscience and heart and life.

Now, here is preaching for to-day. Here is preaching to the exact conditions and temptations of our own life. You have the

minute introspection and analysis of character;
you have abundant emphasis of the value of
the individual soul to God ; you have the
soul wakening to feel its solitary relation to
God, and rejoicing in the purely spiritual
character of religion. Then you have the
plausible temptations — from providence,
from temperament, from example,—to be
satisfied with this and to be selfish ; and you
have these overcome, and the type set of a
substitution and sinbearing, for our task in
fulfilling which we have nothing less than
the grace and perfect example of Christ
Himself.

5. Lastly, I have to speak of the chief
subject for which the preacher of to-day will
study the Old Testament—its theology,
properly so called.

He, who of living students of the Old
Testament has shown the keenest insight

into its meaning, my own revered teacher, has said that its message is summed up in one word—the word God. His witness is true. All that we have been considering derives its inspiration from certain beliefs and ideas about God. The universalism to which the religion attains is due to His sovereignty. The yearning and passion to win men which beat through prophecy and wisdom, the spirit which commands the future, are His zeal—*The zeal of the Lord of Hosts will perform this!* It is because God stands near to men and is interested in all their life, that the doctrine of the Old Testament is so practical, so incisive, so homely. It is because He is omnipotent that the hopes and ideals of righteousness are so certain of fulfilment. The law is but the result of His character. The long history is but His patience and His judgment. The prophecy is the consciousness of His compulsion. The very style of the Old Testament is due to its sense of God. The jealous Deity, who forbade His votaries to express their thoughts of Him in any form of material life, however full of His beauty and His power, or in any work of their hands, however wrought with love and cunning, poured Himself into this literature, into its grammar, its metaphors, its poetry, till in every part it quivers and shines with His Spirit —and we can indeed say, it is His Likeness and His Image.

Now, in this supreme matter, the science of criticism, so far from diminishing the preacher's confidence, has given us a greater assurance. It tells us that the difference between the Hebrew faith and the other Semitic religions, out of which this grew, both as theologies and systems of law and ritual,

is the character of the Hebrew God. It tells
us that Hebrew prophecy is explicable by no
natural laws ; that historical research can
suggest no substitute for the prophet's own
reason for his message—*Thus saith the
Lord.*

It is, then, gentlemen, a Revelation, with
which you have to deal in the Old Testament. This is the supreme thing for you
as preachers. In this is summed up all your
opportunity and all your confidence in the
Old Testament. It is so sure and so satisfy-
ing a fact, that we can rest in it undisturbed
by the many other things in the Old Testament which are not sure, by the some things
which are even unsettling. But it is so solemn
and so awful a fact, that we dare not move
through the domain which it influences
without feeling everywhere, even in the
smallest details of our research and our

report, reverence and carefulness—an exceeding sense of responsibility both to God, from whom it comes, and to man, for whose eternal welfare we are charged with its gospel:

*Unwin Brothers, The Gresham Press, Chilworth and London*

# HODDER & STOUGHTON'S
## New and Recent Works.

---

## THE PREACHER AND HIS MODELS·
### THE YALE LECTURES ON PREACHING, 1891.

By the Rev. JAMES STALKER, D.D., Author of "The Life of Jesus Christ," "The Life of St. Paul," &c.

#### Sixth Thousand.    Crown 8vo, cloth, 5s.

"Vigorous and inspiriting."—*Saturday Review.*

"The ideal portrayed in these lectures is so lofty that it will excite a sense of shame in every preacher's heart. Yet it is so inspiring that no honest man can lay down this book without resolving that his career shall be a crowded hour of glorious life. The lectures abound in striking sayings."—*Independent.*

### BY THE SAME AUTHOR.
#### PRESENTATION EDITION

## IMAGO CHRISTI:
### THE EXAMPLE OF JESUS CHRIST.

Handsomely bound in padded leather. Red under gold and red lines. 7s. 6d. net. May also be had in calf and Turkey morocco, and in cloth, 5s.

---

### THE LATE PROFESSOR ELMSLIE.
## EXPOSITORY LECTURES AND SERMONS.

By W. GRAY ELMSLIE, M.A., D.D.

Crown 8vo, cloth, 6s.

## PROFESSOR W. G. ELMSLIE, D.D.
### MEMOIR AND SERMONS.

Memoir by W. ROBERTSON NICOLL, M.A., LL.D. With Reminiscences by Professor MARCUS DODS, D.D., Professor HENRY DRUMMOND, Rev. JOHN SMITH, M.A., and Rev. JAMES STALKER, D.D. Third Edition. With Portrait, crown 8vo, cloth, 6s.

# JUDGES AND RUTH.

By Rev. R. A. WATSON, D.D., Author of " Gospels of Yesterday," &c.

Crown 8vo, cloth, 7s. 6d.

" Is possessed of great literary merit, and abounds in eloquent passages."—*Scotsman.*

" This is an unusually attractive volume. . . . His pages will give many a valuable hint to the preacher."—*Literary Churchman.*

## BY THE SAME AUTHOR.

# THE BOOK OF JOB.

Crown 8vo, cloth, 7s. 6d.

# Expositions by Dr. Marcus Dods.

## I.

# THE BOOK OF GENESIS.

By Rev. MARCUS DODS, D.D., Professor of Exegetical Theology New College, Edinburgh.

Sixth Edition.   Crown 8vo, cloth, 7s. 6d.

## II.

# THE FIRST EPISTLE TO THE CORINTHIANS.

Third Edition.   Crown 8vo, cloth, 7s. 6d.

## III.

# THE GOSPEL OF ST. JOHN.

Vol. I.   Second Edition.   Crown 8vo, cloth, 7s. 6d.

## IV.

# THE GOSPEL OF ST. JOHN.

Vol. II.   Crown 8vo, cloth, 7s. 6d.

LONDON: HODDER AND STOUGHTON.

# ImTheStory.com

Personalized Classic Books in many genre's

Unique gift for kids, partners, friends, colleagues

Customize:

- Character Names
- Upload your own front/back cover images (optional)
- Inscribe a personal message/dedication on the
  inside page (optional)

Customize many titles Including
- Alice in Wonderland
- Romeo and Juliet
- The Wizard of Oz
- A Christmas Carol
- Dracula
- Dr. Jekyll & Mr. Hyde
- And more...

CPSIA information can be obtained at www.ICGtesting.com
Printed in the USA
BVOW03s1428021213

337918BV00019B/1317/P